MW01006149

Sticky Faith Curriculum

FULLER YOUTH INSTITUTE

Can I Ask That?
Volume 2: More Hard Questions about God & Faith

LEADER GUIDE

A Sticky Faith Curriculum

Published in the United States of America by
Fuller Youth Institute, 135 N. Oakland Ave., Pasadena, CA, 91182
fulleryouthinstitute.org

ISBN 978-0-9914880-2-5

Cover Design: Matthew Schuler
Interior Design: Macy Phenix Davis, Matthew Schuler, Fuller Youth Institute

Copy Editor: Dana Wilkerson

Printed in the United States of America

Sticky Faith Curriculum

CAN I ASK THAT

THAT

VOLUME  **2**

JIM CANDY
BRAD M. GRIFFIN
KARA POWELL

MORE HARD QUESTIONS
ABOUT GOD & FAITH

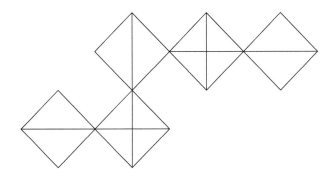

0	Can I ask that?
1	Is it wrong to doubt God?
2	Is hell real? How could God send someone there?
3	Can I do something so bad God won't forgive me?
4	Why do bad things happen to good people?
5	Is sex outside marriage wrong?
6	Why is it so awkward to talk about Jesus with my friends?

Ten tips for reading your Bible   Letter for parents

Can I Ask That?

It was the little things that did it.

Not big stuff like doubting the existence of God altogether, but little stuff. Like hanging out with her best friend from Thailand whose family practiced Buddhism. Or her church leaders' lack of response to two huge back-to-back incidents of racial injustice in national news.

It was the little things that led to Kayla's drift from God.

One of those little things was the way her parents responded when she pointed out things in the Bible that didn't make sense or didn't seem very loving. How could God be all-loving and then damn good people to hell for eternity? Can we do anything that God wouldn't forgive? Whenever Kayla raised a question like this, her parents either flipped out or shut her down with their blanket response for everything: "We just have to trust that the Bible is right and not expect it to defend God to us."

At church it was more subtle. Kayla could see her volunteer youth leaders' inconsistencies in the way they were living outside of church and by what they shared on social media.

She wasn't sure she really knew any people who were living out all the stuff they said they believed. And whenever someone questioned God or a Bible passage in youth group, the high school pastor would respond without really answering the question and then change the subject.

Yeah, lots of little things.

So when Kayla found herself as a junior telling her parents that she didn't want to go to youth group anymore, she couldn't fully explain why. But she knew what she couldn't do: ask questions. For too long and from too many voices, her questions just didn't seem good enough for the church or her parents. Or God.

Or maybe the bigger problem was that God wasn't big enough to handle real questions. Who needs a God like that?

Why this [1]
study?

Research indicates that about five of every ten high schoolers will walk away from the church and their faith after graduation. Like Kayla, many do so long beforehand. Because God deeply cares about each of these young people, the team at the Fuller Youth Institute set out to discover how to help young people develop a faith that lasts—or what we call **Sticky Faith.**

As we learned in our research, there are a variety of reasons a young person might leave faith behind as they cross that bridge:

Some leave because other things become more important to them.

Some leave over a bad experience in a youth group.

Some leave as they seek independence from the opinions of their parents.

Some leave because they never really felt like part of the church to begin with.

> Visit **stickyfaith.org** for more details and all kinds of resources for youth ministries and families.

And some leave because the church fails to handle their deepest questions about life and faith.

These sessions aim to help parents, youth workers, and any adult who cares about teenagers to engage them on a level that takes their developing faith seriously.

Like the first volume of *Can I Ask That?*, this study offers six sessions that explore hard questions we've heard from students and from other leaders who listen to young people.

The study on which you are embarking will be challenging. It was challenging to write and challenging for the groups who field-tested these sessions in their own ministries. These six topics not only will push your students, but they also probably will push you too.

There are few easy answers. You likely will notice points where you're forced to live with the tension of saying, "I don't know." When that happens, remember: **saying "I don't know" is better than avoidance.**

Teenagers will ask these questions with or without you.

Let it be with you. In taking this study seriously, your credibility will increase in the eyes of your students. And, more importantly, the credibility of the gospel of Jesus Christ will increase as well. By being willing to entertain hard questions, you present both yourself and Jesus as safe and trustworthy. Our prayer is that the Holy Spirit will move deeply among your group as you wrestle with some of our faith's deepest and most challenging questions in our day and across time.

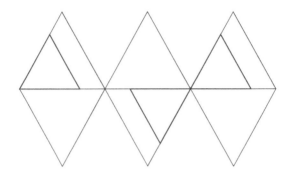

The six sessions tackle the following tough questions:

- ⊗ *Is it wrong to doubt God?*
- ⊗ *Is hell real? How could God send someone there?*
- ⊗ *Can I do something so bad God won't forgive me?*
- ⊗ *Why do bad things happen to good people?*
- ⊗ *Is sex outside marriage wrong?*
- ⊗ *Why is it so awkward to talk about Jesus with my friends?*

2

What you should know
before you start

Here are five important keys to help teenagers engage this study right out of the gate:

> KEY #1:
> *This is about faith that sticks.*

Sticky Faith is an initiative from the Fuller Youth Institute designed to understand and help faith "stick" in young people (see stickyfaith.org for more information and resources). In other words, we want to see young people grow in faith in Christ as they grow into adults. We have observed through research that wrestling with doubt—even doubt in God—can be a very healthy process. We hope this curriculum helps you have real conversations with God and each other about difficult topics.

> KEY #2: *Don't hold back.*

Encourage teenagers that any questions or doubts are welcome. In fact, they are required. Let students be honest. See what God might do in them—and you— through this process. God is not biting fingernails, nervous about the tough questions this study raises. God is also not going to be angry or annoyed by doubt. We have a big God. Since this is the topic of the first session, hopefully you can explore some of these themes more up front.

> KEY #3:
> *Help them learn the "context."*

To understand what the Bible means, we need to understand what it meant for the people who wrote and read it "way back then." Studying the context means discovering who wrote the Bible, to whom they wrote, and why.

For example, imagine a high school student is in class and her phone buzzes. Someone texted her from a number she doesn't recognize:

I've been secretly wanting to ask you this for a while now ... Prom?

Because she doesn't recognize who sent it, she doesn't know whether to be excited or angry. The author and that person's intentions are unknown. Is it a friend playing a joke on her from someone else's phone? Is it the guy she dreams about? Was it sent to her accidentally?

Without the context of this mystery text message, she doesn't know what it means. The Bible is the same way. We need to know who wrote the passage (as much as is possible), why they wrote it, and for what individual or community it was written. Context is crucial for understanding a passage. For that reason, the

"Notes" part of each session shares a little context for key passages.

> KEY #4: Don't send them
> off to question alone.

These sessions are meant to be used in a group, not alone. As a leader, read through the session before you meet. **Let's repeat that: Please read the Leader Guide before each session.** This will deepen your conversation and help you anticipate questions when you meet with the group. There are more tips below on how to lead the sessions logistically.

> KEY #5: Ask God for help.

Leading these sessions will bring up challenging questions and potentially big breakthroughs for you and the teenagers you are leading. Jesus promises the Holy Spirit lives in us to help us make sense of the scriptures. Take God up on this promise, and ask the Holy Spirit to guide you as you lead.

Checklist for leading this study

3

☐ Each student has a *Student Guide* in order to prepare for and follow along during the sessions. We think the physical guide matters because these are questions most people loop back to over and over again, and students will never keep your photocopied handouts. They'll keep a book on their bookshelf, though (it might be one of the only ones!), and maybe even pull it out again a few months or years from now when one of these questions resurfaces and they want to look back at relevant scripture verses and perspectives, and even their own thoughts.

☐ Each student has the opportunity to read through the session *before* the group meeting (this is ideal, but optional). There are pros and cons to sending books home with students. The biggest pro is that they'll be more likely to read the content before and/ or after your meetings, and they'll have notes from your discussion to refer back to. But the obvious con is that they'll forget them and show up without a guide. You might want to decide based on what you already know about your students, or experiment and see how it goes.

☐ Leaders have read the *Leader Guide* and are familiar with the topic and potential direction the conversation may go. Look for the "LEADER NOTES" [In] sprinkled throughout the *Leader Guide* for specific ideas and tips. If you're the youth pastor or organizational leader, you will probably want to gather all of your small group leaders together to talk through the study and highlight issues where your church would want to communicate clearly about particular ideas or positions.

☐ You have emailed parents with a letter similar to the one found at the end of this *Leader Guide*. ***Very important:*** The different opinions surrounding the topics of these sessions can lead to controversy. It is wise to address your intentions for this study directly with parents and other key leaders in your church/organization ahead of time. Also, please note that this study is intended for high school students. Middle school students may or may not be ready for these topics.

Study format

4

Each session is formatted to help students dive into the topic through the following progression:

 Story: A relevant, realistic story designed to get teenagers talking, much like the one at the beginning of this introduction.

q **Questions:** Initial questions to unearth students' current opinions on the topic.

n **Notes:** A dialogue with background context and other factors that influence how people understand the issue. In this section we also share various and often opposing viewpoints within the Christian community or broader culture.

s **Scripture:** Relevant scripture and questions about each topic. All scripture referenced in the study is from the New International Version (NIV) unless otherwise noted, but feel free to use your preferred Bible translation in your small group discussions.

t **Talk:** Fictional conversations that capture the essence of the issue and opinions surrounding it.

A few last things

A few tips for leading the sessions from week to week:

* Each session is designed to take about one hour.

* This conversation guide works way better if your group knows each other before the study. If your group is new or has a few new members who don't know the others well, spend a little time at the beginning on some kind of "get to know you" exercise. Food also helps!

* These sessions are written to help you, the leader, guide the discussion in such a way that honors the theological leaning of your particular tradition. Obviously, express your opinion on each matter, but we encourage you not to short-circuit the dialogue for students who might disagree with your position.

* Read through the opening story out loud as a group to highlight the importance of the topic and spur conversation. Invite different students to read different sections and pose the questions throughout.

* Be okay with saying the words, "I don't know." Be okay with occasional moments of awkward silence as well. Both are important when weighty matters are on the table.

* Resist the temptation to answer every question your teenagers pose. Sometimes it is best to ask them to think more about it or to research their questions on their own. Then offer to buy them lunch and talk about it later!

* You might want to close each session by handing out notecards and inviting

students to write down one question they still have about the topic at hand or any previous topic you've discussed. Sometimes students will share in writing what they don't dare to say out loud. If it feels right, collect these cards so you know topics that would be good to discuss in the future.

* Invite a co-leader to join you. Given the diversity of life experience, tradition, and opinion that probably exists within your church, two leaders can enrich your group's dialogue.

* Consider letting the students know that their friends who don't believe in God are welcome to join the group. In our testing of this study, some students found this to be a great place to bring pre-Christian friends for honest and open dialogue about faith.

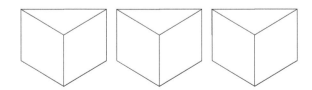

One final note about interpretation: While we've attempted to present well-balanced approaches to these tricky topics, it's inevitable that some of our own biases and beliefs will come through in these lessons. Our own traditions include Presbyterian, Methodist, Nazarene, Assemblies of God, and Congregational backgrounds. We also field tested these sessions and invited critical readers and input from other backgrounds, like Baptist, Evangelical Free, Lutheran, Covenant, and non-denominational churches.

Though our views might seep through—as will yours when you lead your group through the study—our hope is that a variety of viewpoints can be discussed and scripture can be studied in such a way that students arrive at their own views. And while you may go into this hoping students will come out on the other side with "right" beliefs, it may be that the most important part of this whole journey is the process itself.

> That's worth saying again. It may be that the most important part of this whole journey is the process itself.

Finally, lean into God's grace together in the midst of things that challenge your students'— and your own—faith. May we, together with the man asking Jesus to help his son in Mark 9:24, say, "I do believe; *help me overcome my unbelief!*" as we hold faith and doubt side by side.

Session 1

- - - - - - - - - - -

Is it wrong to doubt God?

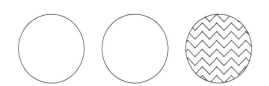

Big Idea

Students will wrestle with doubt's role in their faith journeys.

(leader notes)

Most of these sessions are written with as little bias as possible in order to stimulate discussion and allow students to explore different perspectives. There is also freedom for you as a leader to add to the conversation in a manner that fits your particular stance or tradition. This study, however, favors the perspective that doubt is critical to faith development. We believe this helps open up the context for the rest of the series by freeing students to voice their real—but perhaps hidden—questions.

You'll Need

⊗ Your copy of this *Leader Guide* and a *Student Guide* for each participant.

⊗ A pencil or pen for each participant.

⊗ A Bible.

Terrence's sophomore year was a disaster.

His life was full of challenges that birthed colossal doubts about the existence and goodness of God.

First, there was his friend Ethan. Ethan had struggled for as long as Terrence could remember. Ethan's mom was diagnosed with depression after his dad left two years ago, and Ethan often questioned whether life was worth living. Terrence would never forget the day his friend, Sean, called and told him Ethan had overdosed on pain medication and had died.

Was there something I could have done? Terrence wondered, amid tears.

Then there was Lilly, the girl he had dreamed about since sixth grade. He asked her to the Winter Dance and couldn't believe it when she said yes. Terrence had the big night all planned until he found out Lilly, one of the football team's managers, had hooked up with a junior linebacker on the bus ride to the state playoff game. He felt so betrayed. Why were these things happening?

Is God doing this to me?
he wondered.

Terrence had always heard, "God loves you," from people at church, but the reality of his messy life and a loving God weren't matching up. He very nervously told the pastor at his church that he was having doubts about God. Terrence explained all that had happened that year and wondered aloud why God wasn't helping him out. The pastor looked at him with a bit of shock.

"Terrence, the Bible is very clear about doubt," the pastor said. "The book of James says that anyone who doubts is an 'unstable person.' Ask God to help you, because God loves people who believe without questioning."

Terrence suddenly felt ashamed for admitting doubts to the pastor. *I swear I will never do that again,* Terrence promised himself.

The next week, Terrence was reading for a physics project when he ran across an article titled: "'God Particle' Discovery Ignites Debate Over Science and Religion."

The article described a new type of matter discovered in the universe and quoted a professor saying the God Particle "posits a new story of our creation" independent of religious belief.[1] The article seemed to suggest this new discovery made God irrelevant.

Maybe life is all just an accident, Terrence wondered. *I know my life feels like an accident.*

Terrence didn't know what to believe and had no one he trusted to talk to about his doubts.

 *(questions)*

If you were friends with Terrence and knew what he was feeling and thinking, what would you do or say?

What do you think of the pastor's statement, "God loves people who believe without questioning"? What about his approach to Terrence?

(leader notes)

We will discuss the James passage later in more detail. Try to focus your group's attention on the manner in which this pastor responds by shutting down Terrence's questions.

What kinds of doubts have you heard other people express about God?

(leader notes)

In

It's almost always good to start questions in the "third person" (their doubts) rather than framing them in "first person" (my doubts). It's easier for students to begin talking if it's not quite so personal. But when talking about others' doubts, encourage students to avoid naming specific people and names.

When you question God, which doubt is most common for you? Circle all that apply.

a.   I doubt God exists.

b.   I doubt God is good.

c.   I doubt God is powerful.

d.   I doubt God cares or I think God is angry with me.

e.   I have a different doubt than the ones above.

In *(leader notes)*

Move the question from "other people" to the students in your group and what they wrestle with. We've added some choices to make the question less threatening. These choices typify most Americans and what they believe about God. In fact, a study conducted by Baylor University's Truett Seminary found that about 25 percent of Americans believe God is fully engaged, good, powerful, and loving. The remaining 75 percent of the country agrees with options a-d in the above list.[2]

IMPORTANT: Don't just listen to students' answers. Share your own choice from the list where you are most likely to doubt. It's critical for your group to see that leaders can be honest with doubt; otherwise it is unlikely that your students will feel free to share their own. Remember, some students will begin this study with the belief that God punishes people who doubt. Help them see you model appropriate transparency.

n *(notes)*

A Nervous God

Are there questions that could make God nervous? Some people believe that God will punish those who doubt. But if God is really all-powerful and has nothing to hide, would God fear human questioning? Why would God be opposed to it?

Intellectual vs. Emotional Doubts

There are different kinds of doubts. Some people doubt God because they intellectually wonder if God exists. They often view science and creation as incompatible and can't mentally consent to belief in God. Others doubt due to an emotional barrier. Perhaps something has happened to them that makes belief in God difficult.

> What are other examples of intellectual and emotional doubts? Which kind of doubt do you see in Terrence?

(leader notes)

Examples of intellectual doubts include the origin of creation or an intellectual belief that God isn't really present or doesn't actively take a role in the world around us.

Emotional doubts might include a string of negative events or observations that lead to an emotional response that doubts God. Doubt can also stem from a fear that believing in God might require the person doubting to change her life in a way that feels uncomfortable. Terrence has a combination of both intellectual and emotional doubts.

> Do your own doubts and questions tend toward more emotional or more intellectual issues?

What Does Doubt Do?

Well-known pastor John Ortberg says doubt does important things for our faith journey.

Doubt:

1. makes trust possible

2. adds humility to our faith

3. helps us learn

4. pushes us to seek truth

5. leads to growth[3]

> Which of those five things do you believe is most true? Why?

Does Doubt Make You Unstable?

Terrence's pastor references a verse in James about doubt. He is arguing that doubt is something God frowns on. Take a quick look at James 1:5-8.

If any of you lacks wisdom, you should ask God, who gives generously to all without finding fault, and it will be given to you. But when you ask, you must believe and not doubt, because the one who doubts is like a wave of the sea, blown and tossed by the wind. That person should not expect to receive anything from the Lord. Such a person is double-minded and unstable in all they do.

– James 1:5-8

> What do you think James is trying to say about doubt here? What kinds of doubts is he talking about?

(leader notes)

Let your group wrestle with this, but there are some key points to note:

1. This passage is specifically referencing the request for wisdom and not addressing all doubts.

2. Pastor and writer Earl Palmer uses this verse to make the point that doubt can be good, but "endlessly doubting" is unhelpful.[4]

3. As always, it's important to take any verse and weigh it against the entire witness of the Bible. Never build a theology on one verse.

> Can doubt ever become toxic?

In

(leader notes)

This one is worth asking your group and letting them work it out. Eventually you might offer this insight: When doubt becomes more about the arrogance of the doubter, rather than genuine questioning, it becomes unhealthy. In addition, FYI's Sticky Faith research highlights that doubt can also become toxic for us when we don't share our questions with others and just keep them to ourselves.

> Can certainty about faith ever become toxic?

In

(leader notes)

Students may wonder what this means. You might follow up by asking whether becoming so sure about what we believe sometimes leads to arrogance and to being unwilling to grow in our faith in new ways.

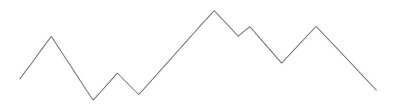

S (*scripture*)

Okay, get ready.

You want to see some real doubt in action? Check out the prayer we find in Psalm 88. The Psalms are filled with prayers that question, doubt, and express anger toward God. These are called laments, and over a third of the Psalms in scripture are like this.

Read Psalm 88:1-9, 13-18.

LORD, you are the God who saves me; day and night I cry out to you.

May my prayer come before you; turn your ear to my cry.

I am overwhelmed with troubles and my life draws near to death.

I am counted among those who go down to the pit; I am like one without strength.

I am set apart with the dead, like the slain who lie in the grave, whom you remember no more, who are cut off from your care.

You have put me in the lowest pit, in the darkest depths.

Your wrath lies heavily on me; you have overwhelmed me with all your waves.

You have taken from me my

closest friends and have made me repulsive to them. I am confined and cannot escape; my eyes are dim with grief.

But I cry to you for help, LORD; in the morning my prayer comes before you.

Why, LORD, do you reject me and hide your face from me?

From my youth I have suffered and been close to death; I have borne your terrors and am in despair.

Your wrath has swept over me; your terrors have destroyed me.

All day long they surround me like a flood; they have completely engulfed me.

You have taken from me friend and neighbor—darkness is my closest friend.

– Psalm 88:1-9, 13-18

What surprises you about this passage?

Is this an example of emotional or intellectual doubt? Why?

 (leader notes)

This is an example of emotional doubt based on hard circumstances haunting the writer. It's important to note the Psalms are full of doubts and questioning God. The prayers in the book of Psalms give us freedom to express our honest feelings and thoughts to God.

Jesus experienced doubt from lots of sources, including his closest friends, the religious leaders, people he met on his travels, and even his own family. (See John 7:5 for an example of Jesus' brothers expressing doubt.)

He also prayed a psalm of lament from the cross, "My God, my God, why have you forsaken me?" (Psalm 22:1, Matthew 27:46, Mark 15:34)

Read John 20:24-29 for an example from one of his closest followers who struggled to believe in Jesus' resurrection:

Now Thomas (also known as Didymus), one of the Twelve, was not with the disciples when Jesus came. So the other disciples told him, "We have seen the Lord!"

But he said to them, "Unless I see the nail marks in his hands and put my finger where the nails were, and put my hand into his side, I will not believe."

A week later his disciples were in the house again, and Thomas was with them. Though the doors were locked, Jesus came and stood among them and said, "Peace be with you!" Then he said to Thomas, "Put your finger here; see my hands. Reach out your hand and put it into his side. Stop doubting and believe."

Thomas said to him, "My Lord and my God!"

Then Jesus told him, "Because you have seen me, you have believed; blessed are those who have not seen and yet have believed."

– John 20:24-29

> What do you notice about how Jesus responds?

In *(leader notes)*

Jesus responds by addressing Thomas' doubts head on, yet without shaming him. Jesus' answer to Thomas' question is not negative. Instead Jesus answers by inviting Thomas close (close enough to touch his wounds!) rather than pushing him away. Then Jesus calls him to trust. In this exchange, doubt led to trust.

Students might also note that in v. 29 Jesus concludes with "blessed are those who have not seen and yet have believed." Thomas could literally see and touch Jesus, while followers who came after Jesus' ascension didn't have the chance to see him in the flesh. So while it's harder to believe without seeing, in some way there is a sense of blessing associated with believing in Jesus without seeing him in person.

If you haven't yet shared any unique perspectives from your own tradition about doubt's role in faith development, now is a good time to do so.

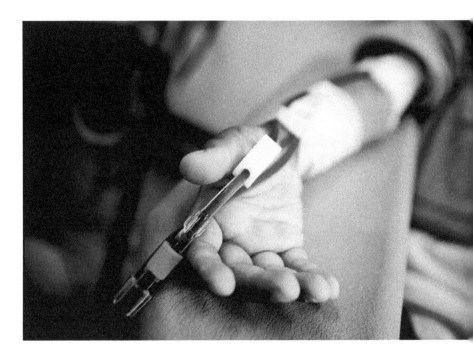

 *(talk)*

Pretend you are with some Christian friends who give their opinions on this topic. Read their comments and write one sentence after each comment that points out a weakness in that person's argument.

DANIA

Doubt shows weakness to people who don't believe in God. If a non-Christian doesn't believe in God and sees Christians doubting, how can we ever expect people to end up believing in Jesus?

JOSH

Doubt is okay, but it should be kept private. My experience with telling others about my doubts isn't good. People end up thinking you aren't really strong in what you believe. It's better to just keep it to yourself.

BRITTA

I think every sermon, book, or conversation about God should be critiqued. My motto is: "Always find the counterargument." My faith is much stronger because I'm constantly using my mind.

MICAH

It's important to be really open about doubt. I like to make sure everyone knows my doubts, so I'm always telling people about them. If people don't respond well, that's their problem.

> List a few people you can go to with questions who will take you—and your questions— seriously. What do you hope you will talk about or do together?

(leader notes)

The book of Job, while a complicated and long story, highlights how important it is to talk to the right kinds of people about your tough questions. Yet even in the midst of Job's repeated tragedies and the poor advice Job received from his friends (several chapters worth!), Job was able to proclaim about God, "Though he slay me, yet will I hope in him" (Job 13:15). Job is a wonderful example of holding the tension of both having doubts and sharing them with God (who speaks back in this case; see Job 38-41), while also maintaining an ongoing sense of trusting God.

Footnotes

1. Chris Lisee, "Higgs Boson: 'God Particle' Discovery Ignites Debate Over Science and Religion," *Huffington Post,* July 14, 2012.

2. Paul Froese and Christopher Bader, *America's Four Gods: What We Say About God—and What That Says About Us* (New York: Oxford University Press, 2010).

3. John Ortberg, *Faith and Doubt* (Grand Rapids: Zondervan, 2008), 135-149.

4. Earl Palmer has great thoughts on this and more in *Trusting God: Christian Faith in a World of Uncertainty* (Vancouver, BC: Regent College Publishing, 2006). For you nerdy types: Palmer argues that the Greek prefix *"dia"* added to *"krino"* (meaning to divide or doubt) gives this version of "doubting" (*diakrinomenos*) an ongoing and "endless" meaning.

Ideas / Notes

Session 2

- - - - - - - - - - - - -

Is hell real? How could God send someone there?

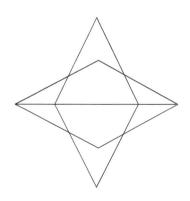

Big Idea

Students will examine the Bible's teaching about hell and judgment, and they will consider the implications for real life, both now and later.

— — —

(leader notes)

This may be your students' first time wondering about this particular issue (and perhaps this is your first time tackling it with a group!). Let them ask questions and raise doubts, and don't be afraid of not being an authority on the subject of hell in the Bible. When your students ask tough questions you can't answer, you can always do some research (maybe through reading, with a pastor, or searching for sources with students themselves) and get back to the group at your next meeting.

You'll Need

In

⊗ Your copy of this *Leader Guide* and a *Student Guide* for each participant.

⊗ A pencil or pen for each participant.

⊗ A Bible.

⊗ Extra sensitivity—this topic and the opening story may be personal for many students.

Gina's grandma died on a Thursday morning.

After days of crying and the family arriving into town, Monday afternoon's funeral was wonderful. Gina's grandma was loved. She was outgoing and funny. Her favorite TV show was *Everybody Loves Raymond*, which endeared her to her grandkids. She was tremendously generous in donating her time to help a local homeless shelter.

At the funeral, the pastor spoke about how kind and generous Gina's grandma was and how wonderful it would be to see her again someday with God in heaven.

Gina's family, cousins, aunts, and uncles all went to dinner after the service. Gina didn't know them all that well because they lived so far away, but she knew her Uncle Chad was "very, very,

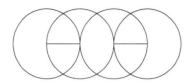

very religious," as Gina's mom would say. Gina got nervous when Chad started asking questions.

"What did you think of the funeral?" Uncle Chad asked Gina and her two sisters.

"It was nice," Gina's older sister Johanna replied, "but sad. I miss my grandma already."

"Do you believe what the pastor said about your grandma going to heaven?" Chad said. "I thought she wasn't a Christian."

It was true. Gina's grandma, while very kind-hearted, made it clear to everyone that she was not a Christian. She didn't believe in God at all. Gina had heard from her mom that a teacher in a Christian school had treated Grandma cruelly when she was a child. It made such an impact on her that she had refused to believe in God's existence ever since.

"I guess I don't really know," Gina said to her uncle, not wanting to get into a debate with him on the day of the funeral.

"Well, I know," Chad replied. "The truth is that people who don't believe in God are going to hell. Your grandma is not going to be in heaven."

Gina's younger sister Bridgette burst into tears.

*Is hell real? How could God
send someone there?*

"Uncle Chad says Grandma is going to hell," she sobbed. Others around the table quickly took notice. It didn't take long before a verbal brawl ensued. Chad's wife even yelled at Chad for being insensitive. Bridgette continued to whimper quietly until her other uncle, Max, whispered to her.

"Your uncle Chad doesn't know what he's talking about, Bridgette," Max said. "Grandma is in heaven now with God. There is no such thing as hell."

Gina loved her church and her student pastor, but nothing they ever talked about had prepared her for this. She started wondering, *Who's right? Is hell real? And if it is, how could a good God send Grandma to hell?*

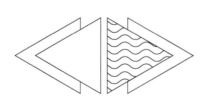

q (questions)

> What stands out to you the most about this story, and why?

In (leader notes)

This story may induce some debate and anger, or it may hit close to home for some teenagers. Pay close attention to what they noticed in the story. In many cases, students' observations about stories and situations are not what we expect. Try not to lead toward a specific answer or response, as you never know what might jump out to a specific student. Be especially sensitive to students who may have recently lost a loved one.

> What image comes to your mind when you think of the word "hell"?

In (leader notes)

Modern conceptions of hell are often shaped by medieval art— fire, demonic monsters, and darkness. We'll get to the biblical origin of the word "hell" in the next section. C.S. Lewis' book *The Great Divorce* paints a very different image of hell. Lewis tells a story of human beings who have chosen to love something on earth more than they love God, and they are allowed to do so for eternity. It illustrates a major point of this study: Hell is the separation of human beings from God. It is not simply God's torture chamber for people God doesn't like. For older teenagers who want to go deeper in this imagery, Lewis' book could be a good follow-up read. Dallas Willard also has a brief but helpful viewpoint on hell in his article "Rethinking Evangelism."[1]

> What do you think of Uncle Chad's opinions and his approach?

 (leader notes)

Students will undoubtedly point out that he takes a cruel and insensitive angle and timing, whether his theology is good or bad. Ask, "How would you have responded to Chad?" And then, "How could Chad have had this conversation differently?"

> What do you think about what Uncle Max whispered to Bridgette: "Grandma is in heaven now with God. There is no such thing as hell"?

 (leader notes)

Let students express their initial opinions about the existence of hell, if they haven't done so already. Resist the temptation to inject your opinion just yet. When you're done here, let your group read through the following "Notes." See what strikes them and spend some time there.

n (notes)

A little vocabulary boost:
How does the Bible speak of hell?

Sheol: The Old Testament word "Sheol" was the Hebrew name for what happens after death. While some Bible translations mention "Sheol" specifically in the Old Testament, your Bible translation might use the word "pit" or "grave" instead. Key to our understanding of "Sheol" is realizing that it always indicated both a place and a condition. Hebrew people did not believe in the life of the soul after death, but they did believe in God's power to ultimately rescue the dead someday. Sheol is meant like an interim state for our bodies and souls after death and before that ultimate rescue. Sheol in Greek is "hades," which is why you see that word in the New Testament.

Gehenna: The word more often translated "hell" in the New Testament is "Gehenna." It was the name of an actual valley near the city of Jerusalem where some ancient (and very evil) kings performed child sacrifices to a different god. It became a hated place, and its name was synonymous with somewhere God would judge. When King Josiah banned child sacrifices to other gods, Gehenna became the trash dump of the town. Fires continually burned there as a way of getting rid of the trash, dead animals, and other refuse that were put there.

Jesus made frequent references to Gehenna, using it as an illustration of ultimate judgment. Some of the passages where Jesus talks about or references the fires of Gehenna include Matthew 11:20-24, Matthew 25:41, Mark 9:43-48, Luke 8:31, Luke 10:12-15, Luke 12:5, and John 15:6, just to name a few!

Why do you think Jesus used Gehenna as imagery for hell?

In *(leader notes)*

Jesus was a master of using concrete things to express abstract realities. He talked about flowers, camels, birds, and other visual aids to help people understand complicated subjects. Jesus specifically chose objects he knew his audience would understand well. In his day, everyone in Palestine knew about Gehenna.

Kind of like when you mention "Las Vegas" in America today, it immediately conjures up certain images or impressions (for example, "What happens in Vegas, stays in Vegas.") Help your group understand that Jesus was, once again, masterfully helping his listeners understand a bigger concept with this term.

What questions do these words and images raise for you about hell and about how someone might end up there?

Choice: God gave human beings the choice to love Jesus and follow God ... or not. At the center of the concept of heaven is the belief that we can be with God forever. Heaven is the place and time where we are with God without separation. Some Christians understand scripture to say that human beings have the choice either to be one of Jesus' followers or to follow something or someone else. God doesn't force humans to follow Jesus. In this way, God gave us "free will." Others believe that God chooses our eternal destiny and we simply live out what God has already chosen.

(leader notes)

In

This is one of the most complicated questions of faith. Do we direct our futures or does God? The concept of choice is important to the topic of hell. If God truly allows us to choose either to follow Jesus or turn away from him during our lifetimes on earth, why wouldn't God honor that choice after death?[2] If you have a little more time here, you might want to ask a question like, "Why would a person who doesn't want to follow God on earth want to spend eternity with God?" to connect with students' ideas of what heaven is like and why we might be motivated to be part of it.

> Would God be good if you were forced to be with God forever ... against your will?

Universalism: Some believe God will save all people. No one has to experience hell, because God's love—the love that resurrected Christ from eternal punishment—overcame death and hell for all of us. A universalist perspective might look at a passage like John 3:16-17 and assert that Jesus did not come to condemn the world, but to save it.

Annihilationism: Some people believe that God will not send people to a place of eternal punishment but, instead, will annihilate their souls so they cease to exist.

In

(leader notes)

There is a theological debate today about whether God allows human beings who have died to be aware of the agony of being separated from God forever, or if God completely destroys souls who have chosen not to follow God. Both sides have their well-known advocates. Likewise, some believe everyone will be saved by God's grace.[3]

It will be natural at this point in the conversation for a student to ask about your church/tradition's perspective on hell and the afterlife, or for you to feel prompted to share. That's appropriate at this point, or you may want to defer it until after you have explored more scripture below.

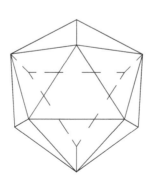

S *(scripture)*

In *(leader notes)*

The goal of exploring these scripture passages is to help teenagers understand two points:

1. God is the judge of humanity. It is never our job to say about a specific person, "That person is going to hell."

2. Jesus spoke very directly about the existence of an afterlife. His words need to be considered.

Read Romans 14:10-13:

> *You, then, why do you judge your brother or sister? Or why do you treat them with contempt? For we will all stand before God's judgment seat. It is written: "'As surely as I live,' says the Lord, 'every knee will bow before me; every tongue will acknowledge God.'" So then, each of us will give an account of ourselves to God. Therefore let us stop passing judgment on one another. Instead, make up your mind not to put any stumbling block or obstacle in the way of a brother or sister.*
>
> *– Romans 14:10-13*

Whose job is it to judge human beings?

(leader notes)

One major victory from this study would be to have your group affirm that judgment is God's realm, not ours. It's important for us to grapple with these questions, but ultimately God—not one of us—will be our judge, in particular when it comes to judgment about our eternal destiny. This is especially important in light of the opening story about Gina's grandma. However, while we are not to judge, God asks us to live out our faith in Jesus in ways that help ourselves and other people grow.

Read Matthew 25:31-46:

"When the Son of Man comes in his glory, and all the angels with him, he will sit on his glorious throne. All the nations will be gathered before him, and he will separate the people one from another as a shepherd separates the sheep from the goats. He will put the sheep on his right and the goats on his left.

"Then the King will say to those on his right, 'Come, you who are blessed by my Father; take your inheritance, the kingdom prepared for you since the creation of the world. For I was hungry and you gave me something to eat, I was thirsty and you gave me something to drink, I was a stranger and you invited me in, I needed clothes and you clothed me, I was sick and you looked after me, I was in prison and you came to visit me.'

"Then the righteous will answer him, 'Lord, when did we see you hungry and feed you, or thirsty and give you something to drink? When did we see you a stranger and invite you in, or needing clothes and clothe you? When did we see you sick or in prison and go to visit you?'

"The King will reply, 'Truly I tell you, whatever you did for one of the least of these brothers and sisters of mine, you did for me.'

"Then he will say to those on his left, 'Depart from me, you who are cursed, into the eternal fire prepared for the devil and his angels. For I was hungry and you gave me nothing to eat, I was thirsty and you gave me nothing to drink, I was a stranger and you did not invite me in, I needed clothes and you did not clothe me, I was sick and in prison and you did not look after me.'

"They also will answer, 'Lord, when did we see you hungry or thirsty or a stranger or needing clothes or sick or in prison, and did not help you?'

"He will reply, 'Truly I tell you, whatever you did not do for one of the least of these, you did not do for me.'

"Then they will go away to eternal punishment, but the righteous to eternal life."

– Matthew 25:31-46

In your own words, what is Jesus saying here?

 In

(leader notes)

Read the passage aloud and let your group write some thoughts before responding out loud. The above question is one of the best ways to start any group discussion—to find out what they understood as a starting point. From there, help them comprehend one of the key points of this study: The Bible's depiction of hell, at its core, involves separation from God. To be apart from God is punishment because it means being separated from the source of every good thing: love, peace, joy, relationships … everything that is good. The closest imagery we have for this is the punishment of "solitary confinement" within the prison system.

In

(leader notes)

It is good to grapple with Jesus' words at face value. In its most direct form, Jesus appears to be saying our treatment of others will determine our future. It is also important to take those words in the context of the entire narrative of the Bible. We will all fail in our treatment of other people. It's important to emphasize grace at the close of this study as students might be aware of their own failure to treat others as Jesus wants us to. Also note that we will pick up on the question of sin and grace in the next session, "Can I do something so bad God won't forgive me?"

How does this teaching line up with Paul's teaching that we are saved by grace, not by works, so that no one can boast (see Ephesians 2:8-9)?

How do these passages help us to better understand judgment and life after death?

(talk)

Pretend you are with some friends who are giving their opinions on this topic. Read their comments and follow the directions below.

ZACH

Hell is not a real place, but a figurative illustration Jesus used. God wouldn't really send people to hell. It was Jesus' way of describing how devastating life is apart from God.

JILL

I was always taught that if I didn't pray a certain prayer and get baptized, I would go to hell. When I was six, my mom helped me pray the right prayer to avoid hell, and then I got baptized at church. I'm all set.

ARIANA

My church is just the opposite. We do infant baptism, and we say faith is from God, not something we do on our own. I don't think I have to "choose" Jesus; he chose me already.

XANDER

Everyone goes to heaven. Hell is just kind of a "threat" to help us behave better. My parents always used to threaten me with punishments so I'd do what they wanted me to do, but then they never actually followed through. Hell is the same idea.

LIZI

I think hell is a real place that people go to if they choose to live a life of not following Jesus. God wouldn't force someone to be in heaven if they didn't want to be there. That doesn't sound like a good God. Jesus seemed to think hell was a real place, which means I do too.

Write a 1 next to the person you most agree with, and then a 2, 3, 4, and finally a 5 for the person you most disagree with. Why did you rank the statements the way you did? Share with others in your group which statement you most agreed with, and why.

What other questions does this study raise for you?

(leader notes)

Take notes on what your students share, as their questions can form the backbone of your next lesson or even series of lessons.

Footnotes

1. Dallas Willard, "Rethinking Evangelism," *Cutting Edge*, Winter 2001. http://www.dwillard.org/articles/artview.asp?artID=53

2. The debate on whether we choose or God predetermines or "predestines" human beings for heaven or hell has raged for centuries (literally). John Calvin is most associated with the doctrine of predestination, which is a central part of "Calvinism." Recent authors following Calvinist thinking include Tim Keller (Redeemer Church in New York City) and John Piper (pastor and writer). Jacob Arminius responded to Calvinism by saying it is primarily our choice to follow Jesus that determines our future. John Wesley and the Methodist movements grew out of Arminianism, and recent authors from the Arminian perspective include Stanley Hauerwas and William Willimon.

3. Rob Bell's controversial book *Love Wins* is worth reviewing for the most recent debate on this topic.

Ideas / Notes

Session 3

Can I do something so bad God won't forgive me?

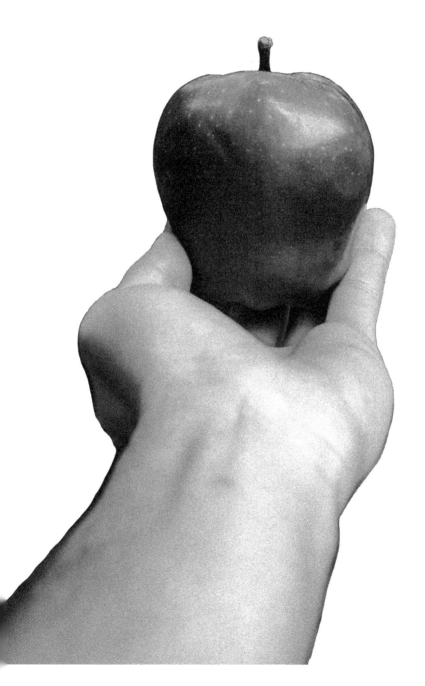

Students will learn that God offers us forgiveness and restoration, even when we make really bad choices.

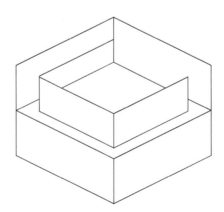

You'll Need

(leader notes)

⊗ Your copy of this *Leader Guide* and a *Student Guide* for each participant.

⊗ To read Romans 7:14–8:2 ahead of time to become familiar with Paul's own struggle with sin and the promise that there is no condemnation for those who are in Christ.

⊗ A pencil or pen for each participant.

⊗ A Bible.

Ryan showed up

to a church middle school program called Fusion in seventh grade. His friend Lars had invited him. Ryan liked the games, the cool and funny leaders, and a girl named Lorna. For about a year, he never missed a meeting and became well loved.

After Christmas break his eighth grade year, April, the youth pastor, noticed Ryan had not attended Fusion three weeks in a row. She asked one of her volunteers, Thomas, to call Ryan to let him know they missed him. For three weeks, Thomas tried to get in touch with Ryan, but Ryan never returned his messages.

"What happened to Ryan?" April asked Lars one night. "We miss him. Is everything okay?"

"Um, yeah ... about that," Lars said. "I don't think we'll be seeing Ryan anymore."

"Why not?" April asked, disappointed.

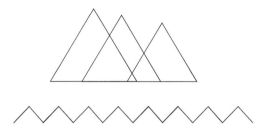

Lars told April what happened over Christmas break. Ryan went to a big New Year's Eve party at a friend's house. He met a group of eighth graders from another school who brought marijuana to the party. Ryan tried it.

"He thinks he's so bad that he shouldn't be at church anymore," Lars said. "I've tried to convince him to come back, but he won't."

April and Thomas kept reaching out to Ryan, but he wouldn't respond. Eventually they gave up.

Meanwhile, Ryan had been feeling guilty. *I know God doesn't want me to be doing this,* he thought. He flipped open his Bible to 1 John 3:9 and read: "No one who is born of God will continue to sin, because God's seed remains in them; they cannot go on sinning, because they have been born of God."

I must not be born of God, Ryan thought. *I decided to follow Jesus last year, and it says I won't sin if I'm from God.*

Ryan felt defeated, and his life began to change drastically after that. He started hanging out with the "potheads," flunked two classes his freshman year, got suspended for punching another student his sophomore year, and started sleeping around with girls his junior year.

His dad, a business exec who was rarely home, threatened to send Ryan to a special school in another part of the state. Ryan tried to apologize and begged to stay.

"If you are really sorry," Ryan's dad said, "you'll stop acting so stupid."

Late in his junior year, Ryan was at a convenience store trying to buy cigarettes after school.

"Ryan? Is that you?"

Ryan recognized the voice and turned. It was April. Ryan felt panic come over him. *What will she say?* he wondered.

"I can't believe it's you!" April said with a smile.

Ryan was surprised. He could tell April was genuinely excited to see him. "It's been years. I've missed you!"

Ryan shifted his gaze. It was hard for him to look her directly in the eye. "Yeah," he said, "I've been a little busy and got sidetracked, I guess."

April decided to take a chance since she knew she might never see him again.

"Ryan," she paused to gain her thoughts. "I want you to know, no matter what has happened or what you've done, God is real and cares about you."

It was impossible to quickly dismiss someone as genuinely kind as April. Ryan hadn't thought about God or church for a long time.

"Thanks," he said quietly. "But you have no idea. God could never take me back now."

(questions)

> What parts of this story jump out to you? Why?

> What factors led to Ryan's statement,
> "God could never take me back"?

(leader notes)

Ryan's case is complicated, but it's not uncommon. Let
your group share what led Ryan to this point. Some factors
include:

1. The common response of "hiding" when we do
    something wrong. Ryan didn't return to the youth group.
    Ever since Genesis 3, human beings have been "on the
    run" when they sin. Bad things can often snowball when
    this happens, as is the case with Ryan's story. Note to
    your group that one of the biggest problems in the story
    is that Ryan stopped talking to people who genuinely
    cared about him. He let shame lead to isolation.

2. Ryan read 1 John 3:9 without the bigger story of scripture. He was too new to the faith, or he simply didn't understand that jumping to conclusions based on one verse—or without proper context—is a big mistake.

3. Ryan's dad reinforced Ryan's belief that he was unforgivable.

> Have you ever been able to relate to Ryan? How?

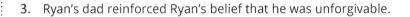

(leader notes)

In

Students may begin to open up some about ways they feel unforgivable. A quick note of caution: As a leader, it can be helpful for you to share some of the things you've felt like God might not forgive you for, but share past mistakes from a posture that puts an emphasis on redemption. Often leaders try to share past mistakes in a tone that glorifies negative actions as a strategy to get students to like them. Also be mindful of the age and maturity level of your students and temper your sharing with discretion.

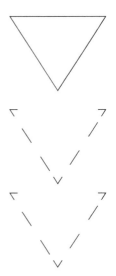

(notes)

One-Verse Wonders

When looking for help in scripture, it often can be tempting to read one Bible verse and see if it gives you direction. Sometimes people jump to conclusions because of one verse. Ryan did this, and the results were not good. When reading the Bible, make sure you read the verses before and after the particular verse you are interested in. It helps to know the broader picture of why that verse is being written and to whom. Finally, almost every topic you find in the Bible can be found in more than one place. Ask someone you trust to help you understand what other voices across the span of scripture might add to the same topic.

Don't Sin Ever Again

Paul, who wrote a lot of the New Testament, is the kind of guy who probably never sinned, right? Well, Romans 7:14-25 is Paul's confession that sin often dominated his life, even after he started following Jesus. Paul talked about the "sinful nature" inside of him that acted against what God's Spirit wanted to do. He described the sinful nature and the Holy Spirit like a "war" inside of him.

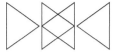

(leader notes)

If you have time to explore Romans 7:14–8:2 with your group, it might be helpful. Or you might want to summarize for them Paul's anguish over the cycle of sin in his own life and the conclusion, "There is now no condemnation for those who are in Christ Jesus" (Romans 8:1). If the conversation leads this direction, you might want to also point out that this doesn't mean we just have a license to sin freely. Earlier in Paul's letter he asks, "Shall we go on sinning so that grace may increase? By no means!" (Romans 6:1-2).

All sin eventually does the same thing: work against the will of God in the world, which ultimately harms others and ourselves.

There are some biblical scholars who believe Paul is describing his life before his decision to follow Christ in Romans 7:15–8:2. If this is your or your church's position, you can point students to other passages that show ongoing struggle with sin even after a commitment to Jesus, such as Galatians 5:17 and 1 Peter 2:11.

What are some things you wish you could stop doing, but you don't seem to be able to stop?

 (leader notes)

This one is probably better written than shared aloud, depending on the comfort level of your group.

Sacrificing Lambs

In the Old Testament, people would kill animals as a sacrifice for the sins they committed. The "sacrificial lamb" was an animal given to God as worship (usually burned on an altar as an offering or way to apologize for the people's sins and make things right. Under the Old Testament understanding of God's law, this animal's death substituted for the person's own death.

Why Did Jesus Die?

Jesus is called "the lamb of God, who takes away the sin of the world" (John 1:29). Jesus' sacrifice is all that is needed to cover our sins. That does not mean you will never sin again. It does mean that Jesus died to forgive you for all the wrong you've done in your past, your present, and everything you will do wrong in the future, too. Jesus' death and resurrection ushered in the beginning of the new creation, and we are waiting for Jesus to come again and make all things new—including us! But between now and then, even in the midst of our ongoing spiritual growth, we still struggle with sin and its results.

(leader notes)

In

If you didn't read Paul's conclusion above, now might be a good time to share Romans 8:1-2, "There is now no condemnation for those who are in Christ Jesus." Also, while we focus here on the sacrificial nature of Jesus' death as it ties to Jewish worship offerings, the New Testament uses a host of other great images to talk about the effect of Jesus' death. You probably don't have time to get into those now, but some other images include victory over evil, legal substitution for judgment, and relational reconciliation.[1]

What does our culture say the "worst" sins are? What have you heard Christians say?

In

(leader notes)

Let students share their ideas. Sometimes we (or church culture) treat various sins as unforgivable. We need to name some of these and challenge the idea that some of these sins are too big for God to forgive.

The Unforgivable Sin

There is one sin that Jesus refers to as being "unforgivable" in Mark 3:28-29. What is Jesus talking about?

In

Get your group to read these two verses together. This is a great chance to see if your group was tracking with the previous "One-Verse Wonders" note above. Hopefully, the group's first response will be to say, "We need to read the verses before and after these two verses to understand more."

Without spending a lot of time unpacking these verses, note that Jesus is being accused of using the power of demons. People are attributing the work of God's Spirit to demonic forces. So it seems logical to conclude given the context of the passage that the "unforgivable" sin Jesus describes is more akin to ongoing and major choices to reject him than it is any one act. (You might wish to share with students about how your church or tradition interprets this verse about the unforgivable sin.) One of the phrases commonly said about this passage is that if a person is wondering if they have committed this "blasphemy against the Holy Spirit," then they likely haven't. Their very curiosity and concern that they have committed that major sin shows their openness to the Lord (which would be incompatible with the serious rejection that Jesus condemns).

How Do We Handle Mistakes?

When we make mistakes—even big ones—Jesus has given us a way to respond. 1 John 1:9 assures us, "If we confess our sins, he is faithful and just and will forgive us our sins and purify us from all unrighteousness." Confession, which just means telling the truth, is a way to be honest before God about the ways we have blown it.

(scripture)

We mentioned Paul earlier. He wasn't always called Paul. Saul was his original name, and he was a key Jewish religious leader after Jesus' death and resurrection. Saul hated that people were starting to believe in Jesus, and it caused him to respond violently. Saul was present when a man named Stephen told a group of religious leaders about Jesus. It didn't go very well for Stephen.

Read Acts 7:57–8:3:

> *At this they covered their ears and, yelling at the top of their voices, they all rushed at him, dragged him out of the city and began to stone him. Meanwhile, the witnesses laid their coats at the feet of a young man named Saul. While they were stoning him, Stephen prayed, "Lord Jesus, receive my spirit." Then he fell on his knees and cried out, "Lord, do not hold this sin against them." When he had said this, he fell asleep. And Saul approved of their killing him.*
>
> *On that day a great persecution broke out against the church in Jerusalem, and all except the apostles were scattered throughout Judea and Samaria. Godly men buried Stephen and mourned deeply for him. But Saul began to destroy the church. Going from house to house, he dragged off both men and women and put them in prison.*
>
> *– Acts 7:57–8:3*

In ancient times, people would kill someone by throwing rocks at them until they died, which was called stoning. That's how Stephen died.

According to this passage, of what crime is Saul guilty?

(leader notes)

Look for the simple answer: murder.

Saul's life was changed when he met Jesus

(that story is recorded in Acts 9). He eventually changed his name to Paul and was the driving force behind the spread of Christianity all across the ancient world. How did Paul view his terrible past?

Read what Paul wrote later in a letter:

— — — — —

> *Here is a trustworthy saying that deserves full acceptance: Christ Jesus came into the world to save sinners—of whom I am the worst. But for that very reason I was shown mercy so that in me, the worst of sinners, Christ Jesus might display his immense patience as an example for those who would believe in him and receive eternal life.*
>
> *– 1 Timothy 1:15-16*

What do you notice about what Paul says in this passage? What feelings does that stir in you?

Did Paul really believe he was forgiven for committing murder? What can we learn from his belief?

It's good to recognize the humility of Paul, who calls himself the "worst" of sinners twice. Forgiveness shows the amazing beauty of God. Paul clearly believed he was forgiven. If God forgives murder, it makes Ryan's offenses look minor. Use this opportunity to affirm to your group that there is no offense that can separate them from the opportunity to receive grace—God's free gift of forgiveness and love.

Don't miss the chance to talk about humility. Paul's admission of guilt and thankfulness to God shows a rare, humble heart.

> Is it possible that Jesus' power shown through his ministry, death, and resurrection is big enough to cover any mistake you could make?

In the Christian tradition, grace is about God's unstoppable love that both forgives and restores us to right relationship with God and others. Many young people don't truly believe that Jesus' power is enough to restore them. It might help to mention 2 Corinthians 5:18-19, that God "... reconciled us to himself through Christ and gave us the ministry of reconciliation: that God was reconciling the world to himself in Christ, not counting people's sins against them."

(talk)

Pretend you are talking with some friends who give their opinions on this topic. Read their comments and, on a scale from 1-10 (where 1 is "totally disagree," and 10 is "totally agree"), rate how much you agree with each person's statement.

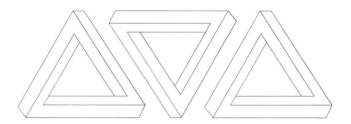

TYLER

I've heard God forgives me, but I don't believe it. Look at how so many people in churches are so judgmental and cruel to other people who have messed up. I can't believe God forgives when people in the church don't seem to do it themselves.

1   2   3   4   5   6   7   8   9   10

SARAH

I'm so thankful God has forgiven me. I don't think I have anything really bad to forgive, but it's amazing that God forgives everything, even the little things.

1   2   3   4   5   6   7   8   9   10

SEAN

As long as I keep trying my hardest to be good, I know God will forgive me. If you stop working at becoming a better person, you aren't really a Christian. It's clear to me that God forgives everything as long as you are making a good effort.

1   2   3   4   5   6   7   8   9   10

AMY

If God forgives everything, I'm going to just keep doing all the fun stuff I feel like doing, even if it's supposedly a sin. Why shouldn't I? I know God will forgive me in the end if I ask for it.

1   2   3   4   5   6   7   8   9   10

How would you respond next in this conversation if they asked you to share what you think about God's forgiveness?

 (leader notes)

You may need to follow up with more scripture to interact with some of these opinion statements. Some helpful passages might include Ephesians 2:4-10 (the relationship between grace and works), James 1:22-25 (listening to the Word accompanied by doing it, not fooling ourselves), and Romans 6:1-4 (we shouldn't sin more just so we can receive more grace; identifying with Jesus' death leads us into new life).

What other questions do you have now about this topic?

 (leader notes)

Make sure you note students' questions so that you can respond to them in future sessions.

Footnotes

1. There has been much debate around the way we understand Christ's sacrifice as atonement for sin. To explore the various understandings of atonement based on New Testament metaphors and how we might talk about them with young people, see Joel Green and Mark D. Baker, *Recovering the Scandal of the Cross: Atonement in New Testament & Contemporary Contexts* (Downers Grove: InterVarsity Press, 2000), and Scot McKnight, *A Community Called Atonement: Living Theology* (Nashville: Abingdon Press, 2007).

Session 4

Why do bad things happen
to good people?

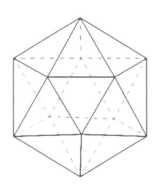

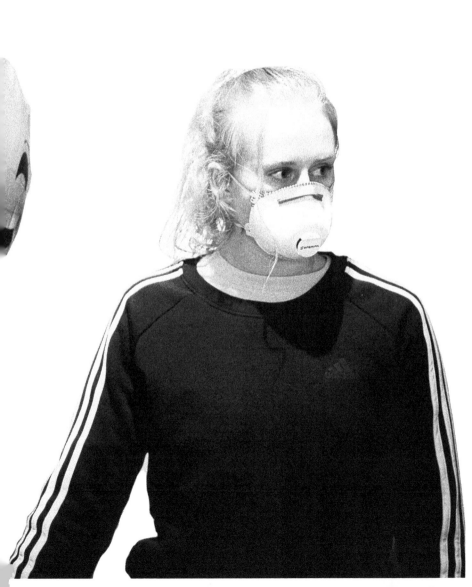

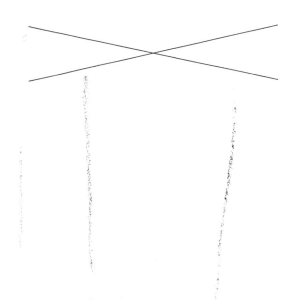

Big Idea

Students will push past easy answers into this tremendously challenging question, and they will consider how God can be good even in the midst of painful tragedies.

You'll Need

(leader notes)

 In

⊗ Your copy of this *Leader Guide* and a *Student Guide* for each participant.

⊗ A pencil or pen for each participant.

⊗ A Bible.

⊗ A piece of paper and pen to draw a diagram.

⊗ A reference for a trained person who can follow up if one of your students shares deeply painful experiences such as past or ongoing abuse, suicidal thoughts, or some other challenging situation that requires trained help after your group session.

Carina will never forget her school's Science Fair Night.

She was a freshman, and her project predicted the year's first snow date based on the last 100 years of data. Carina loved the project and got a great grade, but her memory of the night was forever changed the next morning in her first period science class.

She was running late to school, had forgotten her phone, and rushed in just barely before the bell. Immediately, Carina noticed a few of the other kids were in tears. She also realized her good friend, Jenny, was absent.

"I'm guessing most of you have heard this, but this is a really tragic day." Mrs. Thompson's voice cracked a little on the last word. "Last night Jenny was killed in a car accident."

Carina felt like someone had punched her in the chest. She lost her breath and felt tears burst from her eyes. This news could not possibly be true, could it?

Jenny and her family had left Science Fair Night just like everyone else. They turned down Pine Avenue and saw a car coming at them in the distance. It was swerving all over the road out of control. Immediately, they knew the driver was drunk.

Jenny's dad pulled over onto the shoulder of the road as far as he could in order to get out of the way. They watched in horror as the drunk driver plunged off the opposite side of the road, redirected the car, and came back out of the ditch. The car flew across the road and slammed into the side of Jenny's car.

Jenny died on impact.

Her parents walked away unharmed physically, but they were emotionally tormented. Could they have done something different? Was there a way they could have saved Jenny? They would wonder about these questions for years, battling depression, self-doubt, and anger. Jenny was their only child.

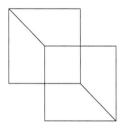

Meanwhile, Mrs. Thompson's science class was also devastated. Jenny's best friend Tanya could hardly speak. Tanya, Jenny, and Carina attended the same church together, and all their lives people had told them things like, "God loves you," and, "God is your shield of protection."

The class sat and cried together in an empty attempt at consolation. But Tanya and Carina couldn't escape one haunting question:

> *How could God love us and let this happen?*

(*questions*)

> Jenny's death was the result of someone else's huge mistake. How do you explain why God allows tragedies like this to happen?

(*leader notes*)

At this point in the session, simply let students talk. Try not to interject much yet.

> What story in our community or your own life comes to mind when you read about this?

(*leader notes*)

Get ready. There is likely at least one member of your group who has a very difficult story to share. Be very aware of who is talking and who might not be ready to share with the entire group. Follow up with students whom you suspect might have something to share but won't do so in a group setting. You may want to prepare to share a story from your own life (appropriate to the context and age of your students) here as well.

What are some of the things you hear people say following tragedies that kind of become cliché phrases? How do you feel when you hear these responses?

How could God love us and let bad things happen?

(leader notes)

An interesting question to ask after hearing your group's responses is: What would the world be like if God didn't allow human beings to choose to do evil? One of the possible implications is that we would no longer have the ability to choose to love God because

there would be no alternative. If God controlled our decisions, would that really be loving? Admittedly, this is an incredibly complicated question without simple answers, but note that this is an angle students may bring up if you do not.

 *(notes)*

Theodicy

It's time to learn a fancy new word. The question of why God permits evil to harm good people is not a new question. People have asked this question for centuries. It even has its own term: theodicy. A theodicy is an attempt to explain the relationship between our suffering and the nature of God.

Many "Theodicies"

People respond several ways when confronted with tragedy:

1. The existence of pain means God is real but isn't good and loving.

2. God isn't powerful enough to stop bad things from happening.

3. God doesn't care and isn't powerful—a combination of the first two.[1]

4. God allows suffering because we are given free will to choose to do good or bad.

5. God must not exist at all (this is called atheism).

6. Evil is a result of satanic and/or demonic powers, and our lives are caught up in a cosmic battle in the spiritual realm between evil and good.

7. Karma is the notion that you get what you deserve in this life based on your actions in a previous life (the belief in reincarnation accompanies this theory).

> Do you or someone you know fit one of the responses above because of some hard things that have happened?

 (leader notes)

Listen to their responses and then be honest with your group. Have you ever believed any of these theodicies? When and why?[2]

> What other explanations have you heard for the problem of the coexistence of both a loving God and our human suffering?

What Sin Really Does

Much of human suffering can be understood more clearly from Genesis 3, the story of the first couple choosing together to disobey God. At the core of sin is humanity's rebellion against God. When those first human beings sinned (and when we sin), four key relationships were broken: our relationships with God, ourselves, each other, and the world around us.

In

It's important for students to understand that brokenness is the result of the entrance of sin into the world. It breaks our relationships in four directions, and we see this clearly in Genesis 3 when Adam and Eve disobeyed and hid (broken relationship with God), when they realized they were naked (broken relationship with self and introduction of shame into the world), when God announced that work would produce thorns and childbirth would be painful (broken relationship with the natural world around us), and in Adam's indictment of Eve as the problem (broken relationship with each other).

Discuss this visual with your group:

While brokenness results from human sin, it's critical to make sure students don't end up believing all suffering is the result of our own individual sin. There are other factors at play, which we'll explore shortly.

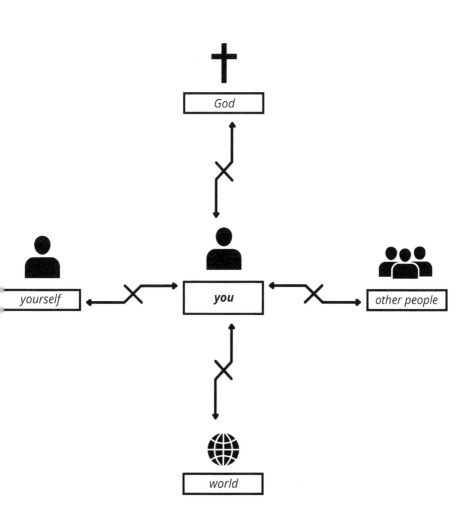

 *(scripture)*

Read John 16:32-33:

> *A time is coming and in fact has come when you will be scattered, each to your own home. You will leave me all alone. Yet I am not alone, for my Father is with me. I have told you these things, so that in me you may have peace. In this world you will have trouble. But take heart! I have overcome the world.*
>
> *– John 16:32-33*

Why are these verses important to this discussion?

In

Jesus says hard times are to be expected. That is an important outlook for anyone who wants to seriously follow Christ. This promise of hard times is coupled with the assurance that Jesus is greater than all human suffering.

Another key passage that often gets quoted in the face of suffering is Romans 8:28: "And we know that in all things God works for the good of those who love him." While this is beautiful and reassuring, it's often used to dismiss very real pain and tragedy. The context of this passage is Paul's assurance that the entire creation will be made new one day, and in the meantime we endure suffering, knowing that ultimately everything will work together for good. That doesn't necessarily mean the events surrounding our particular suffering will simply "turn out for good" in the short term. Our hope is that none of these challenges can separate us from God's love expressed in Jesus, which is described a few verses later in Romans 8:38-39.

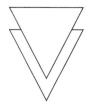

Now read Isaiah 53:3-6:

He was despised and rejected by mankind,
a man of suffering, and familiar with pain.
Like one from whom people hide their faces
he was despised, and we held him in low esteem.
Surely he took up our pain
and bore our suffering,
yet we considered him punished by God,
stricken by him, and afflicted.
But he was pierced for our transgressions,
he was crushed for our iniquities;
the punishment that brought us peace was on him,
and by his wounds we are healed.
We all, like sheep, have gone astray,
each of us has turned to our own way;
and the LORD has laid on him
the iniquity of us all.

– Isaiah 53:3-6

This Old Testament prophecy was fulfilled in Jesus. How does it feel to hear that Jesus was despised, rejected, a man of suffering, and familiar with pain?

In

(leader notes)

Jesus can identify with our suffering. Help your students process that while Jesus may not have faced every specific suffering that we face, he endured the same types of suffering we do, like rejection, betrayal, incredible physical pain, and death. Ask, "Does this change how you pray and relate to God?" Some find it really helpful to know that God identifies with us in our suffering, and he even suffers with us.

You may want to refer back to the session, "Is it wrong to doubt God?" and the use of the psalms of lament as a way to relate to God in the midst of painful circumstances.

Finally, read Revelation 21:4

"He will wipe every tear from their eyes. There will be no more death" or mourning or crying or pain, for the old order of things has passed away.

– Revelation 21:4

> What is this verse referring to? How can there possibly be a day when God will eliminate all suffering?

In *(leader notes)*

Revelation records a vision the apostle John was given about the end of time. These verses illustrate what it will be like when Jesus ushers in a new heaven and earth, and the future of our life with God. Scripture indicates that God will make all things new in this future reality (Revelation 21:5). God's love is more powerful than death. In the meantime, we live with this promise as hope—something we do not yet see, but we trust it to be true. Jesus' resurrection is a sign and promise that one day we will all be raised from the dead and given new resurrection bodies. That's part of Jesus' promise to make "all things new" in the following verse (v. 5, "I am making everything new!").

> Have you ever seen anything good eventually come out of something terrible? What was it?

While God does not cause evil, God sometimes works to bring good out of painful events. Students may be able to name some instances where good has resulted in the midst of awful things, or it may be too soon to turn that corner based on the stories just shared. Don't push it. You, undoubtedly, will have stories to share as well. (Be mindful that your stories are tempered appropriately based on the age and maturity of your students.) Naturally, Romans 8:28 may come up here. Or James 1:2-3, "Consider it pure joy … whenever you face trials of many kinds, because you know that the testing of your faith produces perseverance." God can use hardship to create good things in us and in others. One other example in scripture we can point to is in the life of Joseph, whose brothers sold him into slavery and eventually bowed to him as the leader of Egypt. And yet Joseph came to realize: "You intended to harm me, but God intended it for good" (Genesis 50:20).

Be sure to communicate this message mixed with humility that there is a lot of mystery involved in how God works and in God's timing. We often don't see any good fruit coming from tragedy, but just because we don't see it doesn't mean it isn't happening in others' lives.

(talk)

Imagine you are with some friends who start talking about the question of why bad things happen to good people. Read their viewpoints and write one sentence in each space provided with a summary of how you think that person views both God and suffering.

SHAWNA

I hear Christians say stuff like, "God works out all things for good," and I want to scream. That sounds nice until you are the one suffering. When my parents got a divorce, someone told me it was all in God's plan. Can you believe how insensitive that is?

_____

CAL

I don't understand how God created a world with evil in it. If God created everything, doesn't that mean that somewhere in God, evil exists? I can't trust that kind of God.

_____

NATE

It bothers me when people question God. I had someone ask me once how God could allow a tsunami to kill thousands of people, and I told them to stop questioning God. You just have to trust that God knows how to run things better than you do.

TRAYLON

We can't understand why God allows evil. It's a mystery. I have a nightmare situation I'm walking through right now that I can't even talk about. I hope it's true that God can use things like that for good. I'm putting all my trust into that being true.

Any last thoughts or questions you want to share on this topic?

Footnotes

1. See C.S. Lewis, *The Problem of Pain*, for a more detailed description of these positions. Lewis, who lost his wife to cancer, wrote about God's goodness in the face of suffering.

2. For more ideas exploring theodicy, see Jude Tiersma Watson, "Your Pain: Six Lenses to Help," at https://fulleryouthinstitute.org/articles/your-pain.

Ideas / Notes

Session 5

- - - - - - - - - - -

Is sex outside marriage wrong?

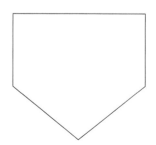

Big Idea

Students will be asked to consider God's desire for sexuality and how that influences their decision-making in their own relationships.

In *(leader notes)*

Similar to the session on doubt, this session leans toward our bias that God designed sex to be best expressed within a marriage relationship, while also fostering an honest discussion with young people about the tough questions they may have about living that out.

You might also want to give parents the heads up that you'll be talking about sex so they can follow up with their own kids if they'd like.

You'll Need

(leader notes)

⊗ Your copy of this *Leader Guide* and a *Student Guide* for each participant.

⊗ A pencil or pen for each participant.

⊗ To consider having a conversation with your church leadership to make sure they know you are tackling this topic and to find out more about what your church or organization believes about human sexuality.

⊗ To pray. Pray for your students to engage and grasp this session. Pray for yourself to have wonderful grace, especially for those students who feel guilt about their past or present.

Trevor's first clue was a text from his friend Walker

jonah's parents told me he's staying @ ur house tonight. can I come over & drop off the money I owe him?

"That's weird," Trevor thought. "Jonah isn't staying at my house tonight." He decided to text Jonah and see what was happening.

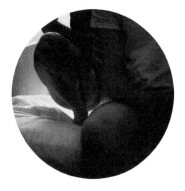

Hey – Walker thinks ur spending the night over here. What's up?

A few minutes later Jonah responded:

I'll tell u what's up later. if my parents call, tell them I'm at ur house using the bathroom then text me right away.

Trevor and Jonah were both juniors and had been friends for over 10 years. This was the first time Jonah had ever done anything like this. What was he doing? Was he in trouble? Why was he hiding from his parents? Trevor decided to text Jonah's girlfriend, Ruthie, to see if she knew anything.

Do you know where Jonah is?

Ruthie didn't respond. Trevor found out the next day what had happened. Ruthie's parents had left town and Jonah stayed at her house.

"We did it," Jonah said with a grin. "Ruthie and I had sex last night."

Trevor tried not to look surprised. A couple of years earlier, both Trevor and Jonah had heard a talk at their church that motivated them to make a decision not to have sex unless they got married. *What happened?*

"We love each other," Jonah said. "We finally woke up and figured out that there was no reason to hold back any longer. Why should we wait? What could be wrong about something so natural?"

q (questions)

What do you think of Jonah and Ruthie's decisions? Why?

In (leader notes)

Sit back and listen. If you have open communication with the students in your group, this should be a pretty fascinating conversation. Let them talk first. Be ready, though, for students who might start off on a very judgmental course. You may need to invite other perspectives if the conversation is being dominated by someone who is immediately writing off Jonah as an idiot (or a sinner or both).

What do you think of Jonah's last comment in the story—"What could be wrong about something so natural?"

In

You will gain points with your group if you acknowledge, from the beginning, how difficult it is not to have sex outside of marriage. One could easily make an argument that it is much more challenging to wait now than at any time in human history. Why? Three reasons:

1. **People are entering puberty earlier**. The average age of puberty has gone from around age 14 a century ago to around 11 years old today. Becoming sexually mature earlier means people will want to become sexually involved with others earlier.

2. **People are getting married later.** The average marriage age today in the US is 29 for men and 27 for women. Fifty years ago, men married at age 22 and women at 20.[1] The culture is waiting longer to marry, and cohabitation without marriage is more common.

3. **Our culture is sex-saturated.** Popular songs, movies, TV, video games, etc., are constantly presenting teenagers with messages about sex. Past generations can't relate to the accessibility of sexual messages that today's teenagers have. Plus, the definition of what "sex" is and what "counts" or doesn't count is incredibly fuzzy for young people today.

Bring these points up with your group, not as a way of saying there isn't hope of abstaining from sex, but as a means of acknowledging the challenge. They will appreciate your honesty.

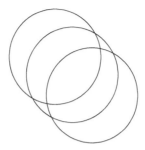

What do you think are the pros and cons of having sex outside of marriage?

(leader notes)

In

They may have already covered this in the first question, but make sure they process some of the physical and emotional cons involved. Potential consequences include pregnancy, disease, and emotional effects. Students may mention pros like finding out if a couple is sexually compatible, or that it's the most powerful way to connect with someone you love. Wait to comment on these statements for now.

 (notes)

Sex Is God's Idea

Don't let anyone tell you sex is wrong. The truth is that sex is God's idea and it is good. In the very beginning God made Adam and Eve and told them (commanded them, actually) to populate the earth—that meant having sex (see Genesis 1:28).

Have you ever talked to God about your relationships with the opposite sex? Why or why not?

 (leader notes)

A big win from this study would be to have students start involving God in their relationships. Praying about both current and future relationships is an enormously healthy practice for anyone of any age.

Sexual Immorality

While there is no verse that specifically says, "Don't have sex before marriage," Paul consistently speaks against all forms of "sexual immorality" (see Ephesians 5:3, 1 Corinthians 6:18, and 1 Thessalonians 4:3-5). New Testament scholars typically affirm that this term "sexual immorality" includes sex outside of marriage.

In

(leader notes)

Take a minute and read the verses cited above out loud if you have time.

Polygamy

Polygamy is a word that means "having more than one spouse." One argument for waiting for marriage to have sex is that God intended sex to be between just two people. If that is truly God's intention, why is the Old Testament filled with men like Jacob, Solomon, and David who had more than one wife? In fact, by the biblical account, Solomon seems to have had sex with over 1,000 women![2]

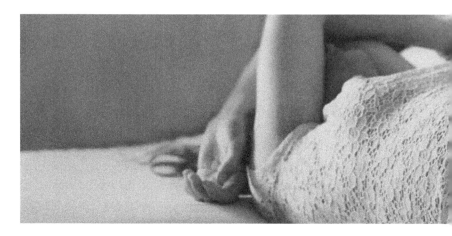

In *(leader notes)*

One could logically argue that some of the Bible's greatest characters had multiple sexual interests, so why shouldn't we, too? Move right on to "One Spouse" below to explore this question.

One Spouse

While the Old Testament took place during an era when men would marry multiple women, that doesn't mean it was God's intention, even though it may have been a cultural norm. Paul (who wrote much of the New Testament) teaches in his writings that marriage is intended to be between just two people in verses like 1 Corinthians 7:1-5 and 1 Timothy 3:2. There are some ancient practices (like polygamy) that the writers of the New Testament condemned.

(leader notes)

In

You will almost certainly have students in your group whose parents were never married, or they were married and got divorced, and then maybe they even remarried. It would be wise to familiarize yourself with your church's understanding of divorce, but regardless of your church's position, we encourage you to highlight God's grace in this discussion.

Covenant

The main way marriage is spoken of in scripture is a covenant relationship. A covenant is more than a promise; it's a deep commitment to be kept until one or both parties die. In fact, both the Old and New Testaments often use marriage as a metaphor to describe our relationship with God. See Isaiah 62:5 and Revelation 19:7-9 for two examples. In this covenant, God promises to be faithful to his vows forever.

S (scripture)

Read Jesus' words in Matthew 19:4-5:

"Haven't you read," he replied, "that at the beginning the Creator 'made them male and female,' and said, 'For this reason a man will leave his father and mother and be united to his wife, and the two will become one flesh?'"

– Matthew 19:4-5

What do you notice about Jesus' words on marriage?

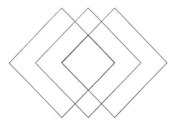

(*leader notes*)

In

At this point students may raise questions about homosexuality and transgender issues. Depending on your group, this may be helpful, or it may turn into a rabbit trail that distracts from other themes in this passage, specifically fidelity and honoring the body (more on this in the next passage below). Please see Session 6 in the first volume of *Can I Ask That?*, where we address "What does the Bible say about being gay?" more thoroughly, for more tips on leading discussions about same-sex attraction.

Now read 1 Corinthians 6:18-20:

> *Flee from sexual immorality. All other sins a person commits are outside the body, but whoever sins sexually, sins against their own body. Do you not know that your bodies are temples of the Holy Spirit, who is in you, whom you have received from God? You are not your own; you were bought at a price. Therefore honor God with your bodies.*
>
> *– 1 Corinthians 6:18-20*

What does it mean that your body is a "temple of the Holy Spirit"?

 (leader notes)

In Jesus' day, the temple was the place where people believed God lived. Jesus and Paul taught instead that God's Holy Spirit lives inside anyone who believes in Jesus. Because of this, Paul said that your body is the new temple.

If my body is God's temple, how far is too far?

(leader notes)

In

Since our bodies are the place where God lives, Paul is saying it is important to treat our bodies well. Sexual sin harms us, and it harms others, who are also God's temples. This is more than coming up with a set of rules about "how far is too far," but it's the question kids want to ask, so we're letting them think about it here. Depending on your style as a teacher, you may want to let students share their own answers to the "too far" question and learn from each other, or you may want to present your own recommendation for them.

In addition, now would be a great time to discuss pornography and sexting. How do these practices help us care for the temple or work to destroy it? Push your group to give reasons for their answers.

One analogy that may work with your group is to compare sex with fire. Fire is an amazing thing when it's used in the context of a fireplace. Take fire out of the fireplace, and it is potentially devastating.

A topic that may come up in this discussion, here or earlier, is masturbation. Because Christians disagree on whether masturbation is a self-focused sin, a divine gift for releasing sexual frustration, or somewhere in between, we leave it to you to handle that conversation within your own tradition and convictions. It's worth thinking through ahead of time how you will respond when it emerges in this session, and it's a good idea to have that conversation separately with boys and girls.

Read 1 Corinthians 10:13:

> *No temptation has overtaken you except what is common to mankind. And God is faithful; he will not let you be tempted beyond what you can bear. But when you are tempted, he will also provide a way out so that you can endure it.*
>
> *- 1 Corinthians 10:13*

Why is this verse important to this particular discussion?

(leader notes)

Here are three great points to ponder toward the conclusion of this session:

1. Other people don't exist for your personal pleasure. It is clear throughout scripture that God does not want us to think about other people in terms of what they can do for us. *(Note: This may be the most important "aha" point of the session for some of your students.)*

2. You will have desires, but you don't have to act on them. This passage from 1 Corinthians reminds us that God is with us in the midst of this challenge. Remind students of your earlier comments about why being a teenager today might be the toughest time in human history to not have sex outside of marriage. Teenagers and adults who make the choice to abstain will certainly need God's help.

3. Sex isn't the focus of life, no matter what the media might say. There are many aspects of a healthy life and healthy relationships that are worth enjoying and that bring great fulfillment to us beyond sex. Jesus modeled this for us in his own unmarried adult life.

> What happens if I mess up, or if I messed up (even a lot) already?

 (leader notes)

It is highly likely that someone in your group has crossed boundaries that they regret. At this point in the discussion, you may want to reinforce that no sexual action is beyond God's forgiveness and grace.

It's an appropriate time to refer back to the discussion in "Can I do something so bad God won't forgive me?", reminding students that Jesus' power and love are bigger than any mistake we might make.

(talk)

Pretend you are with some friends who start talking about sex. Read their viewpoints and follow the instructions below.

ELLA

Not only is sex before marriage wrong, but we shouldn't come close to tempting ourselves. My first kiss is going to be with my husband during our wedding. If we're really going to be pure, like the Bible says, we shouldn't do anything physical until we get married.

PABLO

As long as you're safe about sex, why would God stop us from enjoying it? It's an old-fashioned idea that sex outside of marriage is wrong. The world has progressed and so should Christians.

ABBY

I think you should only have sex with one person, but it's OK if that's before marriage. If you love each other and you know you are going to get married, you should probably have sex with that person to see if you are a true match. It would be terrible to get married and find out you're not very compatible sexually.

JACK

I'm going to get married before I have sex. People think I'm crazy, but I want to share that only with my wife and no one else. It's a struggle to wait, though. My girlfriend and I are tempted all the time.

Which of the above voices most closely represents how most people you know would look at the issue of sex outside of marriage?

Who do you think you'd want to talk with more about their view? What would you want to say to them?

Based on what we've discussed today, what personal decisions would you like to make about sex?

What other questions do you have about this topic?

(leader notes)

Be especially sensitive to students who feel guilt in this area from something in their present or past. Don't miss the opportunity to follow up with those students to assure them of God's love for them (and yours, too).

Footnotes

1. See Census Bureau data from 2014, http://www.census.gov/hhes/families/data/marital.html; CE Copen, K Daniels, J Vespa, and WD Mosher, "First marriages in the United States: Data from the 2006-2011 National Survey of Family Growth," National health statistics reports; no 49 (Hyattsville, MD: National Center for Health Statistics, 2012); and Wendy Wang and Kim Parker, "Record Share of Americans Have Never Married: As Values, Economics and Gender Patterns Change" (Washington, D.C.: Pew Research Center's Social & Demographic Trends project, September 2014).

2. 1 Kings 11:1-3. Note that if you read on in chapter 11, things did not go well for Solomon because of this.

Ideas / Notes

Session 6

Why is it so awkward to talk about Jesus with my friends?

Big Idea

Students will consider Jesus' call to "make disciples"
in light of their own community and relationships.

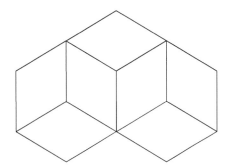

You'll Need

In

(leader notes)

⊗ Your copy of this *Leader Guide* and a *Student Guide* for each student.

⊗ A pencil or pen for each student.

⊗ A Bible.

Kali first started drinking alcohol her sophomore year

when her older sister began giving her cases of beer to share with her friends. Her life became one party story after another. But she always felt like there was something more to live for—something less empty.

That emptiness changed the summer before her senior year. Manny, her good friend from the guys' lacrosse team, invited Kali to his house and said, "I need to talk to you about something important to me."

Kali could tell Manny was suddenly very nervous. Manny started sharing about his faith in Jesus, and he even pulled out a Bible and read a couple of verses. At first it was totally awkward, but then for some reason it began to click for Kali.

"Yeah," Kali said. "My life's a mess. I want to believe in God, and I don't totally understand it, but I want to follow Jesus." They prayed together for God to help Kali and for Jesus to become her Lord.

Kali's life changed a lot. She started

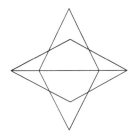

growing in her faith and trusting God. She even started going to a Christian group that met in people's homes to talk about Jesus with other high school students. At one of those meetings, one of the older college student leaders shared how he tried to twist every interaction he had with someone who wasn't a Christian into a "spiritual" conversation. Whether they were talking about football or finals, he figured out how to talk about how much people need Jesus. Maybe it was just his cool beard and easy smile, but he made it seem really natural.

"Jesus wants you to tell your friends about God," the leader said. "Pray right now for who the Holy Spirit wants you to share with. Then come back next week and we'll share some awesome stories about what happened."

Kali was terrified. She thought, *God really wants me to do this? What if I get rejected?*

After praying, Kali decided to talk to Lizi. Lizi was one of her "party" friends, and Kali considered Lizi one of her closest friends. Kali passed her in the hall at school and summoned up her courage to ask Lizi to eat lunch with her so they could have a serious talk.

At lunch, Kali pivoted the conversation from the math test they had just taken to talking about why Lizi needed to follow Jesus because she needed to be saved from her sin, just like the college leader had described. When Kali finished, she looked at Lizi awkwardly, waiting for her response.

"Are you serious?" Lizi said. "This is what you wanted to talk about?"

"Yeah," Kali said. "It's important to me, and I don't want you to be separated from God anymore." She had heard one of the leaders at the group use that phrase.

"I seriously think you must be joking," Lizi said, anger flashing in her eyes. "Ever since you started this 'God thing,' you've changed. And I don't like how you've changed. You're becoming such a freak."

Lizi picked up her food and left Kali sitting alone. She felt embarrassed and confused, and she wondered what she had done wrong.

q *(questions)*

> What did you notice in this story?

> Has anyone ever tried to share their religious beliefs with you? What happened?

In *(leader notes)*

Let them share experiences here. They don't necessarily have to talk only about Christians sharing their beliefs. They may recall someone from another faith going door-to-door or holding a sign by the road. How did it make them feel? Was it a good thing or not? Why? Be especially sensitive if some of the students in your group may not consider themselves Christians. This story might spark anger or bitterness from past experiences with believers, and some of that may need to be shared.

What do you think of the college student leader's instructions to share about faith with someone this week?

 In *(leader notes)*

Help students notice that it's a positive that "cool beard guy" is passionate about seeing other people know Jesus. If you get silence, stir them by asking, "Is there anything about this guy that feels wrong?" You could make an argument that, by pressuring students to share by next week, he is actually urging them to do something artificial. And twisting every conversation to mention Jesus might not feel very natural either.

> Why do you think Kali responded to her
> conversation with Manny positively, while Lizi
> just got angry?

(leader notes)

Different people respond differently to the story of Jesus based on many factors, including the Holy Spirit's timing (which we can't predict or control). Help your group understand that faith is not formulaic. In a deep, authentic friendship, incredible care should be given to sharing Jesus in a way that is personal and that comes from a humble spirit. Kali's comment, "I don't want you to be separated from God," was simply parroting what someone else had said, and it may not have been the best place to start with Lizi.

> Why would anyone feel the need to share
> their faith with someone else? Why not just
> keep it private?

(leader notes)

Let them talk for a few moments here, and then head to the "Notes" section.

(notes)

The Great Commission

Jesus himself is the source of our call to share our faith in God with others. Jesus' last words in Matthew's gospel are often called "The Great Commission" (though Jesus himself didn't use that language). Commission is a fancy word meaning an official task that has been given to someone; at its core this passage is about Jesus sending out his followers to share his message. Check out Matthew 28:18-20:

Then Jesus came to them and said, "All authority in heaven and on earth has been given to me. Therefore go and make disciples of all nations, baptizing them in the name of the Father and of the Son and of the Holy Spirit, and teaching them to obey everything I have commanded you. And surely I am with you always, to the very end of the age."

– Matthew 28:18-20

Do you think this passage specifically says that Jesus wants us to share our faith? Why or why not?

In

(leader notes)

Don't take for granted that your group knows what "disciple" means in this passage. Make sure you mention that "disciple" means "learner" or "apprentice," and it refers to a follower of Jesus in this context. Making disciples of all nations seems to mean introducing people to the good news that Jesus is Lord, as well as encouraging people who are already Jesus-followers to live out faith in their everyday lives through obedience to Christ. It's in this context that Jesus says, "I am with you."

The original tone of Jesus' words indicated something ongoing, so we might also translate this, "as you are going ...." That can mean as you're going to school, to band practice, or to the other things that are part of your normal life, as much as it might mean going around the world.

Evangelism

You've probably heard this word before, but what does it mean? The original Greek word for evangelist meant something like "one who brings a good message." Sharing the message of Jesus, or being an evangelist, is listed as one of the ways God equips people to serve him, also known as a "spiritual gift" (Ephesians 4:11).

> What if I don't think I have the gift of evangelism? Does that mean I don't have to tell others about God?

 (leader notes)

Just because we aren't gifted at something doesn't mean God doesn't want us to do it. In fact, God is continually asking people to do things they aren't necessarily good at. Sharing faith might come easier for others (who may have the spiritual gift of evangelism), but it doesn't mean it is the responsibility of only a few believers.

Gentleness and Respect

The Bible gives us clues on how we should share our faith. The author of 1 Peter is writing to encourage Christians who are hated because of their faith. In the midst of that context, 1 Peter 3:15 says, "But in your hearts revere Christ as Lord. Always be prepared to give an answer to everyone who asks you to give the reason for the hope that you have. But do this with gentleness and respect." Even in the face of being disliked for our faith in God, Peter invites us to share our faith with respect for the other person.

> What ideas does this give you about how you could talk about faith with someone else?

Dialogue vs. Monologue

Another clue about sharing faith is found in Acts 17:16-34. Paul was in the city of Athens where the people believed in many different gods. Paul modeled the type of conversations we can have today by genuinely listening to others. He even complimented them for being "religious" and invited them to notice how their beliefs and openness to spirituality pointed toward Jesus.

If you have extra time, both of these passages are great for additional review and discussion. Ask your group when they have felt that someone genuinely listened to them when they spoke about something that is important to them. What did that person do to be a good listener? How can that help us with others?

> If I'm respectful in telling someone about Jesus and they still reject me, did I do something wrong?

(leader notes)

The Gospels include a number of stories of people, and even whole cities, rejecting Jesus (see Luke 4:16-31 for a prime example) and then later his disciples (there are a number of stories of this in Acts). It is always good to ask God if we are sharing Jesus in the right way, but some people will reject the message no matter what we do or say.

Announcing the Kingdom

The writers of the New Testament Gospels talked about Jesus' mission as announcing the kingdom—or reign—of God. This is the essence of the "good news"—that God is breaking through to us and has, through Jesus, begun making all things new. We live in the in-between time when the reign of Jesus as Lord has begun, but it isn't yet complete. During this season, we are invited to join in God's mission to make all things new. Sharing the gospel—through words, service, acts of compassion, and our very lives—is participating in the in-breaking Kingdom of God.[1]

S *(scripture)*

You've heard it said plenty of times that actions speak louder than words. Words certainly matter, but the way we live reveals our real beliefs, convictions, and values. One of the reasons some people avoid Christians is a perception that believers are hypocritical and judgmental. On the flip side, sometimes people come to know Jesus through discovering a community that loves one another deeply and serves the community and the poor faithfully. As we develop a community that is loving and hospitable, we are sharing Jesus with others by what we do. Here's Jesus' take on this:

A new command I give you: Love one another. As I have loved you, so you must love one another. By this everyone will know that you are my disciples, if you love one another. ...

As the Father has loved me, so have I loved you. Now remain in my love. If you keep my commands, you will remain in my love, just as I have kept my Father's commands and remain in his love. I have told you this so that my joy may be in you and that your joy may be complete. My command is this: Love each other as I have loved you. Greater love has no one than this: to lay down one's life for one's friends. You are my friends if you do what I command. I no longer call you servants, because a servant does not know his master's business. Instead, I have called you friends, for everything that I learned from my Father I have made known to you.

—John 13:34-35; 15:9-15

What surprises you about what Jesus says here?

(leader notes)

If students don't point these things out, you might mention that it's stunning that Jesus suggests believers will be known by love rather than by words or some kind of external mark of membership in a group. Also note that Jesus shifts the power here by calling his followers "friends."

> How does what we read earlier about sharing about Jesus with gentleness and respect in 1 Peter 3:15 relate to Jesus' teachings in John?

> How do you see believers living out these commands today? How can that be a way to share our faith with others?

 (leader notes)

If students come up with more negative examples than positive ones, push them a bit to consider how their own relationships with each other and with others in the church might be signposts of God's presence in the community.

Also, if students have mentioned that they don't know how to talk about sharing faith because they're not sure if they will get it right, this is a good time to reassure them that they can always answer a question with, "I don't know, but what I do know is …" and follow it with why they choose to trust Jesus and why they are part of the community marked by Christ's love. This would also be a good time to share with students about the main points your church or tradition would focus on while telling others about Jesus, and you might wish to help answer some of those questions for which students might not know the answers.

> Has trusting and following Jesus impacted your life in a way that you'd want to tell someone else about? How? What would you want to share?

(leader notes)

This is a good point to actually practice sharing a story with someone else about why we follow Christ. Depending on your time and the tone of your group, consider having students break into pairs and share for five minutes as if they were sharing with a friend who was not yet a believer, and then debrief together how that went. If your group includes those who are just exploring faith, you may choose to simply have a brief group discussion.

 *(talk)*

Pretend you are with some friends who give their opinions on this topic. Read their comments and answer the questions below.

NATALIE

I think it's offensive when people share their faith. It doesn't matter if you're Christian, Muslim, Jewish, or whatever. Just keep your belief in God to yourself and everyone will be happy.

TODD

Waiting until you have a good relationship with someone before you share Jesus with them is just an excuse to put off what you know you should be doing. God is looking for people with the courage to be bold about Jesus and not be so scared all the time.

PHOEBE

I think the best way to share Jesus with someone is just to invite them to church. I get scared about sharing my faith, and the pastor at my church is so great at explaining it all. Why take the chance of messing it up?

TYLER

I hate those guys who preach in public places. They just
make people mad and not want to follow God even more. You
should know someone really well before you share about
Jesus. No one ever follows God because they've
been screamed at.

What person above do you most
relate to? Why?

Who do you least relate to? Why?

How do you want today's discussion to impact
the way you interact with your friends?

Footnotes

1. For a deeper exploration of these ideas, see N.T. Wright, *Surprised by Hope: Rethinking Heaven, the Resurrection, and the Mission of the Church* (New York: Harper Collins, 2008), in particular pp 207ff.

Ideas / Notes

10 Tips for reading your Bible

Hopefully this study has left you hungry to learn and grow more in your faith in God. One way to do that is by reading your Bible. Like anything worth doing, it takes some practice and time to know how to read it well. Here are a few tips on how you can get started or perhaps make your attempts at reading the Bible more meaningful.

1

Pray for the Spirit to Help You

You will not be able to understand the Bible well without God's help. Pray for the Holy Spirit to guide you when you read. Jesus told his followers, "When the Spirit of truth comes, he will guide you into all truth ..." (John 16:13). Take Jesus up on this promise and invite God to lead you. Ask God to give you a heart that is open to being changed.

Formation vs. Information

2

To read the Bible and grow from it, you need to learn a different way to read. In school, you usually read for "information." Reading for school often means you need to read as much as you can, as fast as you can. Why? Two words: FINAL EXAM.

But reading the Bible is more about "formation" than information. God is using the Bible to shape or form you into a new person. That doesn't happen by reading as fast as you can and trying to memorize facts. With the Bible, it's often just the opposite. Read the Bible slowly. Pray as you go. Stop and ask questions. There is no pressure to "get through it." *If you are just trying to get through the Bible, the Bible won't get through to you.*

No Shame   **3**

High school is often the first time people start to feel shame that they don't know much about the Bible. Don't fall into the trap of thinking everyone knows how to read the Bible except you. Many adults, probably even those who go to your church, don't know how to read it well.

Sometimes high schoolers feel like they are so "far behind" when it comes to Bible knowledge that they don't even try. Don't be afraid to be honest about what you do and don't understand about the Bible, and ask for help from a trusted leader (see #7 below).

4 *Get a Readable Bible*

Did you know there are all kinds of Bible translations out there? Make sure your Bible has words that are easily understandable. The *King James Version* may not be your best choice, because it was translated in a language that was popular centuries ago. Some translations that are easier for students to read include the *New International Version (NIV), Common English Bible (CEB), New Revised Standard Version (NRSV), or the New Living Translation (NLT).* Another version of the Bible called *The Message* utilizes modern phrases and expressions to communicate in today's language as much as possible, and it pulls out the verse numbers so the passages read more like a novel. Most of the excerpts in this study have been from the *NIV* translation. You might also want to look for a Bible that has extra notes for context, sometimes called a "Study Bible." Some of these are written especially for teenagers.

5

Don't Start at Start

Jim remembers getting his first Bible, opening it, and starting to read it just like every book he'd ever read; from the beginning to the end. He made it to Exodus before he quit. If you've never read the Bible before, *you may not want to start in Genesis*. Read one of the gospels first (Matthew, Mark, Luke, or John). Those books tell Jesus' story and are a great place to get started. Then go back and get a sense for the bigger story from Creation to New Creation (Genesis to Revelation).

Read the Notes Before the Book

A good Bible will often include notes that introduce each book. It is good to read those notes before you dive in. Bibles with a good introduction will help you understand the context of what you are reading. Context is important because it tells you who is writing to whom and why they are writing.

Bible Reading is a "Team Sport"

When you begin reading the Bible, you will be confused at times. That is okay. Read with someone else who knows the Bible more than you do. Find a pastor at your church, another Christian group leader, a parent, or a friend who knows the Bible and can help you. Don't struggle through the Bible on your own!

Use Your Imagination

The Bible tells some of the greatest stories you'll ever read. It also does not always elaborate on important elements of those stories. When you read stories in the Bible, stop and ask questions like, "What was the person thinking and feeling? What would it have been like to be there?" Use your imagination when you read the Bible.

It's About God

The Bible is not a "nice road map" with good tips on how to live. The Bible is a collection of stories, poems, songs, and letters that work together to tell one big story about God and about us. There are great thoughts about living your life, but the goal of the Bible is to reveal God and to draw you into a relationship with God. Get to know God as you read it.

Stick With It!

Many people start the Bible, get confused, and quit. Don't let that be you. If you are confused, remember that you're not alone. Reading the Bible is much like learning to play an instrument or a new sport. The more you practice reading it, the more natural it will become. Don't give up.

Insider Tips

⊗ There are two major sections of the Bible: The Old and New Testaments. The Old Testament tells the story of creation, of the journeys of God's people, and of their anticipation of the coming of Jesus. It also includes books like the Psalms, which capture poetry and songs that span the breadth of human emotion and response to God. The New Testament tells the story of Jesus on earth and what his life, death and resurrection mean. It goes on to share about the earliest churches and some of their letters to one another about living out the way of Jesus together. It closes with visions of Jesus returning to make all things new, and a promise that he will bring those visions to reality some day.

⊗ The Bible is broken into chapters and verses. John 3:16 refers to a verse in the gospel of John, chapter 3, verse 16. The little numbers you find in the midst of the paragraphs and sentences are verse numbers and make things easier to find. Many Bibles include footnotes that refer you to other passages where you find a similar verse, idea, or an exact quote that is repeated by another author. Sometimes that can help you piece together the different parts of the story.

⊗ The Gospels are the four books that start the New Testament (Matthew, Mark, Luke, and John) and tell the story of Jesus. The word *gospel* means "good news."

Letter for Parents

Here is a sample letter you can send to parents or anyone else you think should know what you will be studying in these sessions. Due to the varying approaches different churches, traditions and organizations have to these challenging topics, we highly recommend you send this before you begin in order to allow for questions up front. Please adapt the letter as needed to fit your particular context.

— — —

Dear Parents,

I'm writing to let you know about an important study we are beginning with high school students.

We will be using a resource titled *Can I Ask That?*, a Sticky Faith curriculum from the Fuller Youth Institute (fulleryouthinstitute.org), that is designed to lead teenagers in critical conversations about their faith. This study will invite our students to look at topics like the existence of hell, why bad things happen to good people, and sex outside of marriage. It raises hard questions that don't have easy answers, and it helps students think about them from a biblical perspective.

We have a conviction that high schoolers should wrestle with challenging topics now, with adults who know them and care about their faith, rather than on their own later. Some research suggests that about 50 percent of youth group participants will leave their faith when they graduate from high school (see stickyfaith.org for more research and resources addressing this concern). We don't want young people to leave faith in Christ because we haven't had real conversations with them about topics that matter.

The studies are written to intentionally encourage students to consider many sides of these issues and help them begin to form their own opinions based on dialogue around scripture, different Christian and non-Christian perspectives, and the tradition of our church. If you are interested in a copy of the curriculum, please let us know. We always welcome your questions and input.

Also, would you please pray for this study? We believe it has the potential to lead to great breakthroughs for a lot of our young people. We'd be grateful if you asked God to help make that happen.

Thanks for allowing us to partner with you to grow and strengthen the spiritual lives of your kids.

Blessings,

Session 4

Jackson Simmer for Unsplash.
Untitled by Flickr user Lauren Rushing.
Move it Driver by Flickr user Mike Babiarz.
Car wreck in front of Manhattan bridge by Flickr user Adrian8_8.
Teenager say yes by Flickr user Mehmet Nevzat Erdoğan.
Untitled by Flickr user Sean Donohue.
Nathan McBride for Unsplash.
Childhood Denied by Flickr user Sergio Pani.
Silhouette by Flickr user Flood G.

Session 5

Alex Iby for Unsplash.
Sex by Flickr user Rupert Ganzer.
Untitled by Flickr user Lindsay Stanford.
Love by Flickr user Hans Van Den Berg.
Carolyn V for Unsplash.
Midday / It's cold out there by Flickr user Malloreigh.
Untitled by Flickr user Silvia Sala.
Young Love by Flickr user Syxrious Sergio.
Sunrise Contemplations by Flickr user Jesi.

Session 6

Chase Fade for Unsplash.
Night Drink by Flickr user Diego Sevilla Ruiz.
Memories by Flickr user Tippi T.
Back to School by Flickr user Nick Kenrick.
Venice Beach California by Flickr user Patrick Merritt.
Summer by Flickr user Basher Tome.
Robert Koorenny for Unsplash.
Locked in his world by Flickr user Hernán Piñera.
And the time stood still by Flickr user Johanna Herbst.
Afternoon Drinking Games by Flickr user Thomas Hawk.

CPSIA information can be obtained
at www.ICGtesting.com
Printed in the USA
BVHW042006100322
631053BV00008B/1344